#travelsend

poems
@
travel's end

Darryl
by
Whetter

Cover image by the author
Author and back cover photos: Gisèle Thériault
Cover concept by the author, executed by Rebekah Wetmore
Editor: Andrew Wetmore

ISBN: 978-1-990187-85-8
First edition September, 2023

MOOSE HOUSE
PUBLICATIONS

2475 Perotte Road
Annapolis County, NS
B0S 1A0

moosehousepress.com
info@moosehousepress.com

We live and work in Mi'kma'ki, the ancestral and unceded territory of the Mi'kmaw People. This territory is covered by the "Treaties of Peace and Friendship" which Mi'kmaw and Wolastoqiyik (Maliseet) People first signed with the British Crown in 1725. The treaties did not deal with surrender of lands and resources but in fact recognized Mi'kmaq and Wolastoqiyik (Maliseet) title and established the rules for what was to be an ongoing relationship between nations. We are all Treaty people.

Also by Darryl Whetter

Fiction
A Sharp Tooth in the Fur: Stories (2003)
The Push & the Pull: A Novel (2008)
Keeping Things Whole: A Novel (2013)
Our Sands: A Novel (2020)

Poetry
Origins (2012)
Search Box Bed (2017)

Edited Anthologies
Teaching Creative Writing in Asia (2021)
Teaching Creative Writing in Canada (due in 2024)
The Best Asian Short Stories (2022)

à la belle Gisèle Thériault,

who was there

even the few times she wasn't

#travelsend

The Luggage-Scale Years

Caelum non animum mutant qui trans mare currunt.
They change their sky, not their souls, who race across the sea.
—Horace

The Luggage-Scale Years

shunning world travel
was so much easier in my tofu days,
when I couldn't afford several flights
and rooms per year. my past
biking to work without ever
quite admitting that *we* can make a difference
but *I* probably can't.   the million dollars a day
my government gives to the tar sands,
our genocidal pensions

I sold a Prius to move to the other side of the planet
and admit to some delusions. to sign my name,
like so many, with a chemtrail
cutting the blue.   packing a life down,
2.5 suitcases and just a few
boxes of mailed books

when you're going to fly 18,000 kilometres for a job
then another ten to keep it, what's five more for fun?
circling the globe every year and a half
after three decades of reusable shopping bags and recycled
toilet paper.   now these battlefield fridges
emptied in my wake.   whiter, vampire coffins
coughing on then off

the shamingly accurate   *SIN*
found poetry of Singapore's airport code, *SIN*,
spat again and again onto my scuffed,
hefted luggage, my 23-kilogram life

Postcards

I have to admit
are finally becoming *past*cards.
searching six stores in Fukuoka, Japan's
sixth-largest city, for these image wafers,
Eucharists of affection, book covers
for semi-private *hellos*
and travel's humble brag, a slower

flip-book social media for the half-
peeping Toms with half a mystery solved,
the *here* so clear if not the *you*
       Wish you were...

shingling café and bar tables
across four continents now.   the few
addresses I have memorized, family and friends
on postal-code speed dial.   the licked
stamp a burr under this thin
intercontinental saddle, the franked
thumbprint of government bureaucracy
yet efficacy

our 4" X 6" quest for Saigon's undeniably impressive
Central Post Office, the arched yellow
windows then ceiling, all those colonial *M*s
writing their lasting
mes, miens, meurtres

Couples, Afoot

travelling together, the not-quite race
to figure out each new shower tap,
reddened lab rat or shrieking vanguard.
the first seismic responder files
reports on mattress and pillow

Act I: drying your face with the bath mat
Act II: walking out and telling her
        that hotel grin

compass and Customs   a giant roulette wheel
confusing the bed sides. a whiter, linen TARDIS
grounding every room, the thrust
stage of touring theatre   the star of every stay
in this architecture of arousal. the soft but strong
tongue of the room. afternoon nookie
while playing job hooky

all
we time
almost no
me. the very
mixed blessing
of a warm toilet seat

the crimson tax of your period
across four continents. the pain
you tamp down in plane, train, taxi or *tuk-tuk*

the other
in-flight entertainment.
swim buddy, bodyguard,
store mirror (though I'm still not
holding your purse).
snore victim and hostage
to the other's jet lag. dining
companion, vista and view.
audience, critic, fellow
balcony Muppet. co-author. a sweatier, footsore
Lennon and M.

sole witness to my triply verboten
cup of Nestlé instant coffee, my
mea culpa cuppa, the Jonestown Kool Aid
of global water tables

the relationship moderate and militant
shift every hour, the plan and the flow:
>   *Have you thought of double-knotting*
>   *that fucking shoe?*

almost all the advice, posts and replies I need
in this nearly complete travel forum
of and for two

Luggage

we pack precisely
because some of our stuff
isn't all.   nomad illusions

the stickered steamer trunks have all sailed away.
suitcases also evolve. the long-suffering handle,
that dog collar or field-cutting yoke,
dropped in importance after the wheels
wheeled in

how well do you?
some pack Russian dolls of delight,
the soul mirror of compartments within compartments
      miniaturized toiletries, a compact
      arsenal to remove moisture here,
      add it there. blister-pack pharmaceuticals, tiny
      ease bullets.   the mesh
      IT centre of cables and chargers

engineers of inner space
covet the hidden chamber
of an empty shoe. snug nest
or bulletproof vest
for some squat jar
or delicate protuberance

condom travellers
put their bags in bags.
no Asian airport would be complete
without its busy
luggage-wrapping machine.   swirling
silver skins of plastic, scuff armour,
alongside ambling Mr. *fuck it all in a bag*

The Ridiculous Travel Mimes of my Husband

that first ruinous restaurant success   *the bill?*
air-scribbled across the glazed diners,
stylus fingers etching the greasy air
over clinking glasses and ossuary plates

his thumb suddenly springing up
in relieved approval. this unexpected
Asian Fonz

then the failures, his pianist's
full octave hands as wide as the chest
of many ten-year-olds in Thailand,
Bali, Malaysia, recovering Vietnam

menuuuuu?   hinged palms prying apart,
upturned, stigmata appetizers
an open book of non-secrets
secreting confusion

a two-fer for two. the three
middle fingers curled in
so up-thrust thumb and a rocked
protruding pinky say bottle
before the peace sign requests   *two beer*
despite a frosty word as universal
as *jazz, taxi, sex*

never the lout's snapped fingers,
that divorce summons, nor the Mason's
sly shake. far from the truly
digital telecommunication of stadium pitcher and catcher
reading their jacked man

how could he?
wife   twirling or tapping a Western
wedding ring then, please no, a trickling
waterfall of all ten fingers past upturned cheeks, tilting
his head about his
who-is-this? chin

hotel lobbies, courtyards, hallways, all that mopped
half-public air unlocked with the same
cranked, pinched, ignition-tripping
key?

we just ate   an incomprehensible
hipster dice throw, a Nike swoosh on the sidewalk
out from his stomach then back
at some penultimate *maître d'.*
a conjuring to dissolve the ready litany
        kebab, seafood, barbecue
        pizza, pasta, curry

numerous
garbled versions of *later*
an @ whorl as big as a bike tire
cranked right, the slight
self-primed uptick and out.
me go bus tomorrow a barrel leap
of arm and vertical
chopping palm.
even more complex, *earlier,*
a ribbon-wristed shunt out
then concave back in. not even I
know that shuttling wrist has travelled
through twenty years of lecture halls
      prolepsis out to the right and
      analepsis tucked back sinister

after a day out to temple or beach,
(the temple of the beach) he even drops language with me,
hand-translating our couple's deep code in jouncing cab,
open-sided *tuk-tuk* or impatient elevator. a hefting
grapefruit palm and drawstring fingers
      water balloon
      full bladder
      me first?

two horizontally V-ed fingers munch their double-cut,
air scissors silently announcing
vasectomy
      the world needs more
      too bad that guy didn't
      I'm so glad I

and, only for me,
(I gamble, I pray, I insist),
tented knuckles reared back toward his tanned biceps
for the adder's determined, double dart,
all fingers springing out straight
then back, once and again.
another, more private question
in the Jack Nicholson leer
at hotel or rooftop bar, there on the roasting beach
and sent with a grin. maybe some crumbling
panko sand, always
from his working hand

Long Haul Flights

a long way down
        after up
the long and not winding road
the end
        of a long-distance relationship's
        temporary celibacy
longitude torn, gobbled, collapsed.
the long reach
        around the planet
the longest
        people live off their phones.
long *roll* flights
        this wheeled life:
        shopping cart to
        luggage to a final
        ambulance
the long
        fenced walk of envy
        up to the sequestered rich
the strung
        trail of litter
        beneath blackout blinds, this flung
        counterfeit night
too long
        in the incubator
        the cough sleeve
        without a shit or brushing
        these claggy fangs.
not hauling anything at all,

not even ass given a pace
beyond our control
long as I
can see John Fogerty's light
and you

Surf School

Professor Spicoli holds zinc and pop classes
Down Under on the infinite
Scarborough Beach,
Scarbs in a sunburnt country
that abbreviates everything.
  Mackers in the arvo?
  McDonald's in the afternoon?

we triply pinkened surf pupils,
newbies on the endless ecru shingle,
so many white and clichéd
shrimps on the barbie sands.
shark biscuits catching more vocab
than waves

no other sport few of us do
or even watch
spills its lexicon, rips such a shredding
verbal curl from the point break to the lip
of the wall to huck giant air then drop
into the slot, the tube, the barrel, running
in the green room after a gnarly
back door, the bomb in a set.
cutting back off wall and rails
before the perfect wave
lets you, god damn,
truly hang ten

a tech simpler than sail but far
more demanding than the wheel. the recurrent
human translation of force. a churning power
we might just
ride home to shore

Plastic Water Bottles

my enemy in North America, the enemy
of my gastrointestinal enemy in Asia.
the clear
clutching fingers
of capitalism's invisible hand,
that force I thought mythical, or propaganda,
until thirsty at any temple or beach. the ice-filled coolers
and warm, smiling coins

the transparent
black magic and tragic
millennial turn, my hollow,
crackling confessions.   the most defining
sculpture of the species.   cheap
but lasting. lasting
and cheap. inflated
avatar of self-interest

crime-scene hotel rooms littered
with the spent shell casings of my empties.
small tracer bullets and larger five-nines
dropped behind

I am become ocean Death
the destroyer
of marine worlds

Birds in Airports

winged, global citizens, refreshing
reminders that not only privilege, love
and trauma flit, shuffle and hustle
beneath the world's highest ceilings, these
architectural homages to lift,
      the yonder sky

Pearson, JFK, Heathrow and Changi
all summon these smaller, distant
cousins of the wing. the spirit
animals of aviation. guest-star
wilderness amidst the perfume
and couture. their high,
streaked view of the infirm
wheeled about by the uniformed. the yanked
children with their holler faces,
wide mouths Momma Bird
never need feed

My Man's Back

afoot, I'm behind too often. following
if not chasing a sweaty back
as broad as a cupboard door
I have to worry he's shoving,
not trekking, through Asia.   down
the jungle path and through
the market throng. his rented tan and axial
Dimples of Venus lost invisible
to soaked shirt, groaning knapsack, haste
or annoyance

brisk, receding tombstone. my, yes,
occasional riot shield.   neither of us ever admits
a gun rack if he had to.
almost always my jib sail
never my main

a courtship and love abreast
back in the West
before the narrow paths of steaming
monkey jungle, terraced rice paddy
or flooding crowd force
only one forward

Sweat

a deliquescent *un*superhero, the hidden costume
coming out, the private, humid
contrail of your Asian travels
and life. that slick fashion accessory
at too many meetings. the sudden
sidewalk decisiveness or flooded lassitude

how to save Asian face with dark sickles
spreading under your arms?
every shirt comes two-tone, the possibly
dark front and certainly
dark back. paintbrush hair and the white
palimpsest of dried salt

you pay for this self-inundation
in yoga studio, spin class or bedroom
yet endure your own exploding soak
on Jakarta sidewalks, Cambodian trains, that recurrent quest
for the perfect nasi lemak, katong laksa or rendang.
your face a wet ledger
transcribing chilies, latitude and sun

Travel

probably never more part of the problem,
save it's all problem now.
mitigations only, from and for
our cancer-cell species, DNA's elusive 1%,
the endgame of the starburst long game
as global plastic, selfish genes, crippled forests and choked
rivers reveal the tragic flaw of evolution.
            given ecosystem enough, and time,
every successful species becomes a parasite

unlike Obama's bailout banks
we are not too big to fail

the *lingua franca* of the resort hustle,
not any poem I know,
neither bedroom joke nor Instaspiration,
only the island hotelier's credit-card wisdom
reminds me
            happy wife
            happy life
his practised smile and immaculate shirt

our inequity long weekends, where all trips
are guilt trips

the environmental metastases and my midlife
bank account, waistline and worry

we planeload hordes, with our viral privilege,
plead with an Augustinian god of carbon expenditure
and coral bleaching,
>   *make me good*
>   *but not just yet*

Sinners in a Holy City

the floating, baritone *azan* has been our flung
pilfered soundtrack, if not quite call to prayer
or Madonna,
in Java, Bali, the seaside alleys
of Malaysia's Penang and Mersing,
abstemious Malé

mellifluous if not melodious and undeniably alluring
even for two hyper-educated atheists, a balm
in the sweat of travel. gargled beauty pouring
from the emerald minarets. Ariadne's threads of faith,
municipal charm. the spilled syllables even more fluvial than French.
immune to noise restrictions and gender equity. a curled
urban message soaring
on the pigeon of song:
        continents, millennia, dust
        eternal.
        far from Kansas,
        my darling Toto

Rubber Sole

the metronomic
often maddening
soft tock
of yet another
flip-flop

Trip Advisor

a global village
you want and don't. pure
Groucho Marxism
all these members
    making me never

too similar, too different, too
       crowded, busy, still.
       spicy, bland, expected, conformist.
       too Russian, too Chinese, too smoky, too male.
       strong, weak, rugged, hard on the kids.
       expensive, accessible, popular

ego advisor, ego curator. vector
       and display. these half-naked
       prejudices, vendettas, hang-ups, embedded
       microaggressions.
       so screamingly neurotic
       so privilege drunk,
       go get a vasectomy
       snip advisor

if we're really being honest, sharing this
room with a review,
how many stars would you
       should you
give your own soul?

How Do I Love Me Travelling?

let me count the ways:
Facebook, Insta, Snap and Tik.
posting, tweeting. all these press releases
to and of the self. updating feeds
around the world's
daily contest for food

media-centre knapsacks:
selfie sticks, those magic wands of narcissism,
drone cams a vanity air force,
        my eye in the sky
        only has eyes for me

by *professional travel blogger*
do you mean *Slacker with ADHD but Dad
really kills it at the firm?*

the usual collusion, the standard
marriage of marketing and self-image,
when *Eco-Tour* is really *Ego-Tour* or maybe
just a blood-alcohol level.
        Does anyone who swims
        with bioluminescent phytoplankton
        in Thailand, Vietnam or Cambodia
        do it sober?
long, dollar-a-beer cruises. everyone
shooting their own
underwater pixels

Screaming Baby Air

the postmodern tube, the cylinder
graduated with class, hope and tedium.
the striplit jet, the twentieth-century lever
into the twenty-first.   the species
coming of suicide age

ripping through fluff-dune clouds, all that
can't you think of anything better? cotton.
tugging your own contrail, that climate-change cut mark.
each plane a needle inching the sky's maxed dial.
tip the azure, cobalt and cerulean
into embered garnet, umber aflame, sparking
yellow above the scrim
and the inverse constellation
of city lights
          forsaken below

galley slaves to our own ambitions, ridiculously
free and privileged. the hypnotic hours of small screens,
crammed plastic, smudged aluminum, upholstered
row after row. all those two kinds of people:
the glance back and ease seat recliners
and the catapult dickwads, the *me-firsts*
not too far from a #metoo

each of us thumbing the injection
down the window calibrations, plunging
a chemical pleasure we all know
proves lethal in the extreme

hence the crying babies
who know we shouldn't,
don't need to, would be better not to,
torn from restraint

Beds 1, Guests 2

we're all lazy at
       and afraid of
something

travel
       and your lover
sees it all

I'm Never More White in Asia Than...

on the back of a scooter,
the chevron of my pink
windswept knees. vectors of consumption
and accidental prosperity piloted
through the thrumming weave

when sweating so much
my sweat sweats.
when I am my own miasma,
        rainforest, thunderhead

when thinking of labour rights
and safety equipment, seeing the brown
flip-flop feet up on the indigo
second-storey I-beam, observing the endangered
species of ear protection

when using a knife with my fork,
not a spoon or the ever
clicking sticks

thinking one location warrants one
or maybe two selfies, not this new
stop-motion animation of self. when a conscientious
objector to the selfie Olympics

being ignored by soldier, cop or guard
on subway or at checkout, when never showing ID.
when only glancing at hotel security if I want to
        in this dress-code skin

agreeing with the octogenarian
four-foot Chinese auntie who hockey-boards me
at the subway doors, shoving aside
        the imperialism, the opium wars, the atomic
        sky split open, that spilled yolk

than saying *four-foot*, not 1.2 metres

when price-list women
solicit me in the sidewalk crowd
below dim, narrow staircases.
facial massage to my face then
full body expertly at my passing shoulder or back
        feel good

when not always thinking
what my mother would think

when called *ang moh* and *gwai lo*
to my *ang-moh*, *gwai-lo*, 1.8% of the population face

in the glaring questions of my skin
Where are you from?
How long have you been here?
        Just how fucking great
        is your career?

when addressed first, or exclusively,
when out with my wife, knowing the taxi uncle's
And what do you do, Sir?
will have no sequel for her

in my diamond bullet atheism, my flying
        spaghetti monster

with my cloth bags at the grocery-store,
recycling and missing composting. the whole
Whole Foods checkout optimism
and delusion

than *Boss! Boss! Boss!*
so shamefully hailed.
          Taxi! Khebab! Satay!

on the toilet. busy with bellies
of Bangkok, Bali, Delhi.   the parliament
of my intestines and their liquid
no votes. the panic that even my shit
needs to take a shit

with the endless Facebook escort 'friend' requests
this latest edition
of mail-order brides

Abandoned Bicycles

that less intentional urban sculpture,
locked rust.   the wheels
two dry question marks:
     what happened?

the black tires, cartoon shadows
anchored to the sidewalk, stretched
behind some hasty exit. the derailed
derailleur a seized asset,
a casualty of migration.
packhorse and fellow soldier forsaken
behind the enemy lines of change

desertion in an exoskeleton. a lockjaw
lock. a faithful
dog or horse cold without its master's hand

a tubular widow, a ghost
hauling stiff chain. the rebuke of rust. the cogged
gear wheel chorus. metal smiles
once glossy with lube
now chapped and cracked

the slow escape.
pressure pumped into tires
and your owner. two large
rubber stopwatches marking
the marooned time, some final
corner turned

Air YouNMe

Exhibit A in the disruption, the acceleration
of hive-mind acceleration. broke
gig-economy designers racing
from kitchen-table idea to air-mattress
guest in a week when, cue the irony trumpets,
a design conference overtook San Fran

the second proof, though swipeless,
that the pocket computers we call phones
were always beds waiting to happen.
isolated rooms or whole apartments
springing open for coin

if only my readers and romantic ex-partners
reviewed me so glowingly.   *a Superhost of the soul*

finally the sexagenarian and septuagenarian Web revenge,
the *a-ha!* of the empty nest. international parents and grandparents
renting out those *perfectly good* rooms waiting for you here at home.
the widows and widowers
parcelling out the empty days, grateful to redo
the cleaning, maintenance and (quiet)
rule they once resented

Down Under our smiling, helpful, wine-country host
instantly haunts us both. his
my late wife and *leave you to your privacy*
detonate inside us with our rare but full fear,
hints of the abyssal *after*
lurking in a temporary home

Learning To Dive (when you do have tanks)

the underwater virginity, at least,
we do in stages. take textbook quizzes, follow
the demonstrations, the bubbles and fins, of a certified instructor

an unnatural balance in a natural world
that doesn't want me. sucking
compressed air into my lungs and around them, the engineered hug
of this black, inflatable thorax. all the dialed, sopping
sink and rise. handheld elevator buttons
for water or sky

slip into that elusive zero-G, a true
stationary float you've only found above
in the purest moments of love

slide, seal-slick, above your neoprene buddy
to see the shocking, forgotten transparency of air
in their fat periscope bubbles. silver-edged. cleaner,
empty jellyfish. mirror glass wriggling free
from the black backing below

the near total camouflage of a small octopus
in coral, all that variegated brown
suddenly distinguished by one blinking eye. the slightly uncanny
variations in form. corals of mushroom, cacti, crooked fingers
pointing at you in naked bone

and the bleached dead. underwater forests
petrified or clear cut. another landscape singed
by climate change and sunscreen by our
experience greed

Bullet Train

you always remember your first
time in this second
way to whip through the kilometres,
to liquefy the passing
landscape.   stream it now,
beside not below.   actually see
Japan's crawling green hills.
join the mile-fast club,
the *Alta Velocidad Española* or France's
original *Ligne à Grande Vitesse*

why exhale so much more?   coughing
up, up, up and away   when you can set turned
steel feet into the sprinter's starter blocks and exceed
any speed you'll ever hit in a car with almost no
blood on the tracks

or murky sea water lurching further up each
jagged beach.   do not add
more muscle to every storm.   tropical boxers
training in cages that ready them
to break free

Passport

the ultimate note from Mom.
hall pass, Get Out of Jail Free,
the hockey cards of citizenship
passing you from port to port
or the Medieval
French castle door
         passeport

the national tattoo
we can leave in a sock drawer.
the commonplace book translating
headlines into visa restrictions. the proud
bearers of Singapore, Japan and Germany
stride past the rubble postcards of Syria,
Afghanistan, Iraq, their *access denied*

the flat
Mount Everest of forgery, the best
tailoring many of us will own. the inked
arms race of barcodes and holograms.
that inscribed yearbook of the First World War.
the telegram America sent a sundered world. *Wanted*
/Not Wanted posters from the new
sheriff in town.   the twentieth-century proof
of age yet footnote to Nehemiah, the travel bible
inside the Bible.   flip books of national propaganda photos,
Canada's last spike driven by mutton-chopped white men
not the dynamited Chinese. and of course churning
Niagara Falls   the centrefold of the nation

Expat versus Migrant

another guilt stamp on the pale
passport of my skin

blogs, headlines and sidewalk sandwich boards,
the insurance industry, dating apps, I'm told,
all zip our white skin
into a package labelled *expat*
while the smash-thumbed
Bangladeshi construction workers, slipped-disc
Filipina nannies and Thai toilet scrubbers:
      migrant workers all

chasing the hot remit, funding
a forsaken home while building or maintaining them
for the global rich. a full country of halved women
fund their distant children
by raising another couple's.
      the bright
      and the shadowed,
      the nanny exchange

parts of me cling to Rushdie
      the stereoscopic gaze of the migrant
guilt-proud to finally feel
the cops and soldiers cradle and feather
warm subway triggers in a skin
never my own

train-station lessons but still those double-pump
Paul Bowles syllables tempt and allure,
all that *expat* sweat, linen and gin,
the luggage and stretched love.
a journal, books, a scuffed camera
and a warm bed all the home you need.
apartments again, not houses.
            when you no longer own a drill,
            you stop needing to make holes

here in part because it's not there. no,
we have zero interest in 'buying' a thousand-dollar table
at Singapore's Canadian Expat Ball.   though I do endure
Mustafa Centre's crowded escalators, this Asian
Honest Ed's, ascending from the boneyard of brown shoes
past pink fairyland dolls, dutiful car wax and enormous
aluminum pots, rice bags bigger than pillows,
to dip myself in the amber of home:
            Québec maple syrup

despite the germs of subway, shop and coin
I still finger that tawny taste
as soon as I'm out the door, transported
from Little India's *roti prata* streets knowing
tongues don't believe in clichés

Star Bath, New Zealand

the top of Mount Lyford at the bottom
        (forgive my entrenched northism)
of the world

another pair of oblique islands
share an angle around the world
from our Nova Scotia home. both hang halfway
between the burning equator and melting pole,
between European land grabs (*Nova Zeelandia*)
and Euro-baffling flora and fauna
        (whither the moa).
only the kiwi
airplanes and hotels greet you
with the greeting of their Indigenous
        kia ora

another accurate travel rumour:
the South Island *is* better, the endless
serrated mountains, verdant valleys smudged
and jostled with, yes, an army of sheep.   puffy
white erasers rubbing the endless
hilled green

crank that steering wheel left then right on these skinny
cat-string roads, in this transmission pentathlon of a country
to climb the grey mountain shale and scree.
push fear, hope and engineering to scale Lyford
(and Gaston's Mount Appetite).   risk a puncture
or backward slide for an outdoor bath beneath the stars,
a wood-fired hot-tub for two.   a wet
fractal island outside an off-grid hut
beneath the pricked pour of the Southern night sky,
that way station to the heart
of the Milky Way

ease four legs (two of them hairier) into that steel, chambered heat
for the stacked bath of water below and the dense
slosh of stars above

Packing

playing cards and our running score, gin
rummy across half-a-dozen countries, then half
as many continents. three sizes of bandages. Ziplocs around
flight pens. one book and a spare, the right hand
and the left. journals.
a corkscrew and a small
knife for limes. a few elastic bands, their handy
constriction. ample
ibuprofen. the Frisbee you will use more
as plate or tray. the mitigators
and self-absolving naiveté:
       the nylon shopping bag,
       the reusable mug, that one
       good Tupperware
over the high-carbon miles

pyjamas. you'll wear their soft hello
more in hotel than at home, chill wear.
evening T-shirts.   be sure to take a spare
for your cotton-covetous wife, her grinning prerogative

an army in fact
marches on its gitch

an HDMI cable, stretch
that Netflix fix. whatever chargers
your woman's prosthetic requires:
        contraband in the Maldives,
        Bangkok street fare,
        somehow turned on
        in your heft off the luggage
        belt in 'Nam.
        a knapsack buzz and vibrantly
        blushing love

diarrhea meds and electrolytes, small
pills for the small, wounded room.
those cramped days of pumped
alien heave

the reading glasses you keep
denying you need until maps,
tiny train schedules in Phnom Penh
or Queensland Light Rail. package instructions
on the necessary
pharmacy score

all this
        doing to undo

Chaos People

There really were, Donk had often thought, and thought again now, two kinds of people in the world: Chaos People and Order People. For Donk this was not a bit of cynical, Kiplingish wisdom to be doled out among fellow journalists in barren Intercontinental barrooms. It was not meant in a condescending way. No judgment; it was a purely empirical matter. Chaos People, Order People. Anyone who doubted this had never tried to wait in line, board a plane, or get off a bus among Chaos People. The next necessary division of the world's people took place along the lines of whether they actually knew what they were. The Japanese were Order People and knew it. Americans and English were Chaos People who thought they were Order People. The French were the worst thing to be: Order People who thought they were Chaos People.

—Tom Bissell

Southeast Asia

grouped sweat, coastlines, scooters
and hustle. a sea-licked jungle
of chilies, rice and adaptation

a contemporary label slapped on
by the acquisitive West. a neat classification
for the other side of a shrinking planet.
millions of unwhite people, just so many
Pentagon calculations: fuel then megatonnage
then cheap
factory labour

Singapore, that rule book and
garden city. Indonesia, a necklace of 17,000 islands,
dots and dabs as the Pacific runs turquoise
into the Indian and proud
on a Muslim chest.
Malaysia, sibling in faith,
champion of corruption. the jealous boyfriend
who dumped a young Singapore
then watched her thrive, the blossoming
girl next door, with her defiant
coin-bright eyes

Vietnam, one long beach and hangover
from oppression: France, America, a Communism
that still finds *The Socialist Republic of Vietnam*
taking visa payments in US dollars, bomb tickets.
the lush
coastal destination Thai tourists should actually visit,
to avoid the sales pitches the grim king never hears:
　　　　massage, taxi, tailor!
and so much more

lonely Laos, the only landlocked forest green,
and Cambodia, these poorer cousins at the ASEAN table.
proxy victims of US bombs and landmines.
overgrown craters and under-developed
amputees

Myanmar and Thailand, a history of kings
studying Buddhist peace
while slaughtering and enslaving their neighbours, stealing fat
statues of serene wisdom. smelting and resmelting pilfered
holy gold. undoing then redoing
the same rotund smile in our jungle temple
not yours

The Things They Carried (on scooters)

speed hope resentment endurance, three
to four people, generations, pairs of worn
rubber flip flops

micro-harvests of rice, ginger,
coconuts, fragrant curry leaves
bundled square, one thousand fragile
quotidian eggs, caged ducks, a snorting
pink hog

sleeping toddlers

burning cigarettes and suspended plastic bags of *kopi*
hot or cold, the occasional silver bullet
of an open beer can. an entire restaurant
a sidecar of red hot coals

another scooter
rolling meta-

trailers groaning under
       a pond in a pyramid of blue
       water cooler jugs. frozen parabolas
       of rusty rebar. three
       gun-metal grey
       water buffaloes
       fencing their cage

tropical pragmatism.
we have lanes; they have asphalt
in places

wads of dirty
American money
and white people.
genocide tourists

amputees. the long
short brown arms of US
and Soviet landmines, scorch marks
from a cold war

a unique prism for teen friendship
how deep the driver dips in the curve,
how and where the rider's hands
encircle or avoid

micro minis, johns
sweating in the rear

blocks of ice. smaller, faster
wagons going down the street.
Hey. Hey! a wagging pinkie down low
then a mimed toke up high, the rare
offer of weed in Asia

engagements, exam results, *I got the job!*
hearts   bursting with hope

a long rifle held upright
with pride and purpose, the summoned
teen marksman earning the farmer's respect
and pay

the fluttering
darting hive mind
of the traffic bee, the individuated
node in the swarm

as much freedom
as they can carry and the world
      can burn

Bali

that flower behind the ear,
male or female. each in skirts
and pride, for their swelling, trickling
island of temples and that rarest of resources:
bottom-up culture. traditional costumes a privilege
not a prickly burden. the sidewalk offerings,
weekly processions past the teak carver and up
the soft steps of emerald rice paddies

wide-eyed statues
a bestiary in stone. ululating dragons, shrill,
impish monkeys. sentry lions draped or wrapped
in black and white gingham,
the ubiquitous *saput poleng*, patterned dualism,
the *Rwa Bhineda* balance, a world away
from any race car's checkered flag

where we have stoplights, they have statues.
every major intersection a sculpted
burst of myth.   gypsy taxis circle sun-baked Rama
and his getaway chariot, chattel Sita
and snatching Ravana. 20,000 temples
on a diamond-shaped island
no bigger than Canada's PEI

directions are dynamic: *kaja* is up
to the nearest volcano or *kelod*,
down to the (demon-sluice) sea.   nothing as static,
as pedestrian, as north and south

not just a Hindu island in Muslim Indonesia,
but a home-cooked Hinduism.   religion of water
and the family clan. more tourist charm
for travellers shunning or fleeing family,
         the misperception and disrespect, the dysfunctional
co-dependence driving you to a sea-soaked paradox.
sun-kissed, surf-licked, freedom seekers who are often free
         for walking out of a clan

behind the Intsapix of Bali bliss, no temple
reveres the local water Mafia, the midnight
blocking or cutting of pipes for the few
Western owners, the *subak* revenge

Tri Hita Karana and a decent mojito.   whittled
penis sculptures in a country that just outlawed
premarital sex.   the jade
land of three-fold harmony
with nature, spirit and (the right) people

two hands clasped to heart centre
before a bow and still the most heartfelt
suksma   thank you
you'll ever meet
         suksma mewali

Smoking in Asia

the Wild East. individualism or coiled
brute force in the crowd.   I'll do what I want
with my lungs and yours

the gateway drug
of toil. counterfeit energy
even more portable than *kopi* or chai.
scrolled contracts. white fence posts
dividing pay from health

the methadone of colonialism. old habits,
addictions and spending patterns run deep
after the English forced the Indians to grow
the opium they forced on the Chinese.
Victoria's scorched
breath of victory

some kind of Confucian heat logic.
            take it inside. truly
            enter the dragon

the ubiquitous footprints of today's vaping Chinese,
the concentric smoke rings of their travel.
carless Malay diving villages stock
Coils! Charger! Mesh!   shop uncle
huddled over wire or burner

when population density, coastlines,
colonialism and inequity make you
the thin edge of the climate-crisis wedge,
the beachhead for another cooked tsunami,
    what's a little smoking death?

Cambodia

chaos people, understandably.
cratered. mudslid. Pol Pot a pure thug
compared to sky-dreaming Uncle Ho.
one-quarter of the population lost
not so much to civil war as civil
genocide

history has never looked more like a luxury
than in your misplacing Angkor Wat, all that carved
precision-fit stone lost for half a millennium

the Khmer oh-so Rouge. blood
their terrible cleanser. a two-decade *Animal Farm*
in the steaming jungle.
Sihanoukville's coastal resorts razed for decadence,
punished beaches.
the brief triumph of the uneducated, incels hatching
the cardinal ruler's mistake,
trading rice for guns before the republic's
bullet parsimony and artisanal violence.
Comrade Cain slaying State Enemy Abel.
warm, tired club and hot
wet knife

the *killing fields*, the haunting phrase you gave the world
before competing 'national'
brands of beer advertise, in English,
> *My country, my beer*
> *National beer, national pride.*
a canned alphabet not your own

Angkor Wat

a Hindu temple
repurposed for Buddhism, recycled
slave labour. all that lashed and barged stone
before the phones.   the stooped necks.
tenth-century slaves then sunburnt Western kids
updating, whining and liking,
Instapilgrims photobombing
this excessively bombed country

Pub Street, Siem Reap. the crowded,
dollar-a-beer flip side to the world's largest temple
of temples. UNESCO, that global liquor baron,
barker on the lurching sidewalks:
        scorpion appetizers, teen desserts

tucked in the jungle for 500 years. once the largest
city in the world.   10 million chiselled bricks
lost and overgrown. architectural, spiritual
money in an old coat pocket

all those hauled slabs
abandoned by a Khmer
hauling ass.
build it, and they will come
to steal. your shelter and canals,
that imperviousness to nature
but not nurture, the fists
and bladed steel

little
        remembers like stone

Angkor

whatevs
what time do the Pub Street bars open?
what ya gonna do with your life?
what a world
     a life
what did you do alone in the jungle
     for 500 years?
what about love, Temple,
     don't you want someone to care about you?
what's on your flag
what you can leverage with pole, tide and tyranny
what a *we* can find in *your* backyard.
what's the American dollar doing as a second currency
     when the US dropped more bombs here than on Germany?
what happens to all those fifty-dollar a day temple passes?
what an example
     of slave labour.
     a wet end   then a dry
     slow rebirth
what happens when your neighbours covet your water
what's happening to Canada
     as America gets thirsty

Plastic

mute and matte a Mobius
strip molecule, an atomic snake
eating its own tail. the planet's engagement ring
for a homicidal marriage

the twentieth century's dirty
DNA sample.   the oil industry's seventh-day work.
single-use the word of the year in 2018,
a full five after *selfie*
in this condom life.
        give us this day our daily

cyanide capsule of the species.
all species. a tragic flaw even more murderous
than America's Second Amendment.
a suicide note written in the invisible ink
of convenience. the slippery slope:
cheap, industrial, ubiquitous,
choking. every weak strand
braided into a noose jerked tight
around the Earth. impregnating snowflakes,
raping the rain

the Pacific gyre, a true
United Nations, pocked
mirror of modernity. our Frankensteinian
wretch, even cheaper
and dumber
than Amazon bullets. an ocean-dumped
truckload every minute

trace the world.   the border lines
are now plastic. shampoo bottles, the spent
cartridges of tampon applicators, insistent
greens, greys and blues, dull
orange flames
the high-water mark
of the free market.   every single inch
of Phú Quốc's five-kilometre Bai Truong Beach
has a brittle scum line of bottle, container or cap.
yesterday's bite marks

Singapore

a kind of success
a balance-sheet life.
report cards then bank statements
in reliable black and white, a national
refutation of grey

the Switzerland of Asia:
quadralingual coffee hub and humourless
banking powerhouse. immune to corruption
yet swollen with secrets and offshore money.
a small, neutral, independent nation
with obligatory military service.   every man
primed to muster, fieldstrip and achieve

long past its colonial *sling*
at the Raffles Hotel 'long bar'

Order People who demand a world
of Order People. a city, island and nation
of accountants lost to meta-work. an hour
for your task then 1.5 to document
and justify. each HDB apartment block a vertical
prison yard of rules.   yet the women in your life
will never be safer

what other *gahmen* would block YouPorn
but permit brothels? just another sweating
migrant worker, *lah*. ostentatious Orchard Road,
        shops by day, Prada, Hermès, Salvatore Ferragamo,
        the trillion Apple
before Orchard Tower comes alive
in the vampire night.   the building
Lonely Planet, Trip Advisor and Wikipedia
all call *four floors of whores*

the only other rebellions are culinary, not infidelious.
chili and garlic the ambassadors for whatever works.
the plate a rare chance
to colour outside the lines

the one place I've encrypted my writing, locking doors
of apartment, home-office then hard drive and cloud

amidst the perpetual construction sites, the skyscrapers
a rapier tournament of architectural envy,
sidewalks burn in the Hungry Ghost Festival
while the ghost of Dr. Chia Thye Poh
haunts every rule book.   physicist and MP
detained for 32 years with neither charge nor trial,
that rare political prisoner who can say *amateur*
about Mandela

Canada's national crop
a hanging offence amongst the *kiasu*,
the people most in need of some inhaled relaxation
and skunk. Lamborghinis racing between island stoplights.
generations of accomplishment and planning,
National Tree Planting Day since '71,
yet 1 in 7
          mentally ill

Selfie Sunday

gender and class roles as segregated and oppressive
as the Middle Ages.   Singapore's moated
island castle

Jesus isn't kicking any money lenders
out of the CBD temple   still the oligarchs begrudge
this decency sabbath.   a single, nation-wide
day of still hammers, piling dishes and screaming toddlers.
the Singaporean parents briefly parenting,
self-sequestered inside townhouse or flat
from the temporary flood
of temporary workers
in every outdoor walkway, riverside and park.
the knuckle-scarred builders and groped,
derided nannies and maids, the floor sweepers
and sleepers
        inside, outside
        serfin' SEA

migrant construction crews baked
in generational heat, the high-steel climbers,
boot-trod Bangladeshis and Sri Lankans.
cast(e)-off Indians climb actual ladders
while across town their Singaporean brethren scale professions,
medicine, finance, IT, never knowing what it's like
to step Sunday-free
from heavy boots filled with sweat, gravel,
plaster and blood. proud
in day-off jeans. shirt collars and beer cans
open to the day

contour maps of class, clan and snobbery.
the picnic huddles, the Thais (self-)segregated
from the Filipinas, their blanket and tarpaulin islands
on a small island.   portable
speakers for handphone deejays
with painted or smashed nails
as the afternoon meals give way to dance.
          half an hour
          owning your own hips

despite the strut and twerk, the lager and Pinot,
there is little United Nations matchmaking on this hot
money staircase.   *here* higher than *home* but far
lower than *they.*   the master's retracting
seventh-day leash, the snatch of Sunday warmth,
these habitual
hired smiles

The Birth of an Air-Conditioned Nation

way station between Dubai and Dachau,
genocides direct and indirect. life-saving
death tech. another *have/have-not*
twentieth-century museum piece.   slip another
assembly-line bullet into this electric game
of planetary Russian Roulette

chilled summer movies by the 1920s then the Florida migration
of late-Seventies winter grannies, the Reagan sweet spot
without the sweat.   the slippery
lifeline of the tropics.   democracy and compressors
spreading around the world. the colonist's 'sedan chairs,'
Penang's 'Strawberry Hill,'
traded for condenser and fins, schematics and whir

that climate-crisis object lesson in *me, not we.*
the coiled straitjacket of the home, the seeming
oasis of temporary cool. thumbing down today's temperature
      before I up tomorrow

the physicists' cool
hot debate between compressed or condensed matter.
'phase transitions' in hydrochlorofluorocarbons
then the species.   these oblong white boxes,
Asian wall fridges,
Springsteen's wetter, cooler
     suicide machines

The Singapore River

meandering
signature of maturity.
poster child for an adolescent nation.
the wet transformation
from swamp to entrepôt
in the nineteenth century then from dump
to tourist chute in the late twentieth.
       central planning
       running clean

former latrine, farm ditch and Davey Jones's locker
for abandoned fridges, rusting rebar, whatever the godown,
goddamn, couldn't unload.   a three-kilometre lifeline
choked to death past the *belly of the carp.*
the young republic's original artery
       nearly closed

early Temasek, that trading post
between India and China, then,
       evolutionary milestone or mutation,
landing place for the true
British Invasion. looting
white rule but Conrad's
most important post office in the east,
       today's expensive Fullerton Hotel

a topographically deep harbour
and a politically free port,
a beacon for eternal
human desire   the river
a snaking prelude to the first
telephone system in Asia, that other
Singapore grip

today the bumboats
ferry only tourist cameras, sunburns, dehydration
and jokes.   at night, the oil-slick river
no longer wears the rouge
of glowing red lanterns, though opium ghosts
still sail and pole
up the umbilical cord of a country
now determined
to hang you for weed

Your Application

to write a Singaporean poem
has been rejected
by your loyal and efficient servants,
the Ministry of Culture, Community and Youth's
National Arts Council's
national organization Poetry SG
and its subcommittee
        of professionals!
the Poetry Committee Committee

you are welcome to attend a meeting
about the meeting of the parent Committee Committee
but not its junior Poetry Development Committee

provided you file the *Application
For Unsuccessful Poems*, in print and online,
on the sixty-eighth Wednesday before the Creative
Creatives Creating Creative Creative
sub-committee meeting

mandatory documentation includes
but is not limited to ...

Tekka Market

Singapore's wettest
wet market. a smiling, bustling
slaughterhouse in tile, a labyrinth
of hock and shank under a hanging
canopy of muzzy Asian heat
strip-lit with dutiful fluorescents and cut
by swooping mynas
roiling in the blood funk

the king-pile fruit vendor
fights to maintain his Baltimore corner,
a hard sell on the sweetest
       lychees, mangoes *Thai or Pakistani?*
       the pulled toes of long grapes, the hairy
       testicular rambutans

the border of fruit. a final inhalation at the last
outpost of sweet before the hacked
alleys of meat, the blown
CSI scene of goat, and flies. dull pink mutton
just inches from wool

the seafood vendors truly earn
the slick title, their dripping
basins of snapper, foot-soldier grouper, drilled threadfin,
shy pomfret, the stout logs of snakehead, cables of needlefish,
packed and repacked in ice. the toss of tray, shovel or tub.
their rubber boots, yet your sandals
above a floor of standing water
roped in pink.
the splayed hands of small rays and clenched
fists of crab. the stacks and rows,
the still marine eyes
     precursors to coin

Sweat and (Groucho) Marxism

Asia:
heat, cigarettes and selfies,
filial piety the recurrent curse.
older colleagues supposedly right
just because they're older. HR departments ruined
by duty, male deference and saving face.
boy-men with Ferrari money
still living with Mum

what other country has mandatory state ID
with a mandatory field for "race"?
Better, and worse, that Singapore accepts
only four answers.
     Chinese, Indian, Malay,
     Other
the national
     portrait in a word

vitriol in the hawker-centre spittle.
Go back to Vietnam! This is Singapore.
Sing-a-pore!   the assumption
that my white skin will assent
to cash-register auntie's endless invective
before I, too, walk away from her scalding
     Dirty! Dirty!

Wine Country

hectares of barley simply never say
romantic getaway.
the vodka industry cannot make
potato mounds sexy

the leafy, heliotropic
contact high for couples.
let's scrap the pretense (along
with that neglected spittoon) and add dating
to the wine country van tours.
   I hope you like your morning toast
   as buttery as West Coast Chard

Pinot noir: a genre of red
and relationship memoir. every vineyard
fertilized by a secret corpse

the sacred double alchemy:
photosynthesis then fermentation,
different in degree but not kind
from chugging and body shots.
a sun-dappled, lychee-nosed buzz
is still a buzz. ethyl alcohol a molecular
common denominator

a vine row's top comb of green leaves,
sun spangled from Kelly
to lime as shadow
and light stretch their gradations,
   sea, fern, hunter.
leaves
the size of your niece's
reaching hand

in sunny fields the small grapes grow
between the pleasures, row on row

Salang Boatman

barefoot, nearly toothless, brown eyes
with broken yolks, cornea bleeding into white
after a lifetime of bright water.
  Tioman Terry on his worn pink flyers.
his boat's plastic dashboard has no instruments
or dials save an engraved, Arabic prayer.
  Dremel piety

his fibreglass skiff just a few feet
longer than the aluminum row boat
of fishing pond dreams, Canadian Tire commercials
or Keji memories

his empty pockets and our thirst
slip one island bay for the nearest coastal village,
the—be honest—liquor outlet, despite clouds
  darker than spilled ink.
in open water the waves, I can feel
my white-knuckled wife thinking,
grow in frequency, not just height, speeding
toward us, how?, from five different directions

Half now, he announces at the relieved
sight of an emerging dock.   ashore we scurry for gin
then village kebabs, wave to him as he buys cigarettes
and the fuel for home, lights one
before the other

no sooner have we slipped painter then back-alley wharf
than he cuts his own throttle, weather eye spotting
a school boy at the end of the large ferry pier

white shirt, book bag and patience.
Terry inches closer, chucks his chin and calls in Malay,
assuring us, *I know him daddy*
without looking back or down
to the rented rectangle of our rain cover.
his eyes firm on the boy scrambling
down slick concrete steps then half-soaked old tires,
      the same village support
      in the Maritimes or Malaysia

Pot Cookies on Koh Rong

> The traffic police in Cambodia
> are incomparably corrupt.
> —*An Otherwise Forgettable Travel Guide*

you can't be twenty
on Neil's Sugar Mountain or,
really, tenured and forty-seven on Koh Rong,
Cambodia's car-free, weed-cookie island

lured by rumours of white beaches
and ubiquitous weed, taking, naturally,
the bar-stool advice of a Swedish fireman
we met over six-dollar bespoke cocktails
in Phú Quốc, Vietnam's own island beach,
        wafting, yes Bartender, smoked rosemary
        over smoky Lagavulin

which became the next trip's jostling ride
on an old Blue Bird school bus
denuded of its seats. the better to cram
in backpackers and their enormous
eponymous packs. a hotel run in coastal Sihanoukville,
a clown car of gear and bliss seekers, my one
wheeled suitcase cumbrous on the unsafe bus
then worse on the less safe ferry

two of the twentysomething island seekers amble aboard
        hold the hipster phone
caked in dirt. once-white tee-shirts stained
to dry tea bags.   on strike against showers
they settle in beside me with their funk
and, tease it out, story

English motorcycle mechanics roaring
across Asia. CC brothers for day after day
of Pakistan's roasting desert heat or camping,
as live picnic TV, for five, seven, nine, large Indian families
with busy cell fingers

having only one lever into this baking
Zen and the Art of convo I ask
about the "incomparably corrupt"
Cambodian traffic police.   *Oh*, they smile,
full-throttle,
We haven't stopped
for a traffic cop
since Germany

Expat Liquor & Plants

for Robin Hemley

then they go, again,
contract nomads with spacious luggage
and smudged passports.   back
to gay marriage and freedom of the press,
to clown governments that at least
stopped calling it *manpower*.
to not being a guest,
or needing permission. to owning, not renting,
          digging in

these fast friends you've watched sweat
over two or three years of shared drinks,
face-melting meals, *sotto voce* jokes,
recommendations, exasperation and guilt

all taxes tidied and mouldy
books shipped. the final, rented heat
of a restaurant meal in the quick
equatorial dark before whatever drinks we can
in apartments stripped bare. a wet séance
for hope and memories amidst the long
walls denuded of art. tundra floors
free from the yoke of furniture

we drink
in a naked echo chamber on mismatched
balcony chairs inherited from the last tenant
then left to the next

the clean, bare fridge
clocks a final cold sentry
for our ice alone while the last
gasp of air conditioning gets wasted,
just this once, when we must,
must,
step out onto the steaming balcony
and stir a skirmish of rented thermals
before the certain heat
of a final embrace

Instalment-Plan Littering

George Town, Penang, Malaysia.
street art, literary festival, UNESCO and rats.
almost no bars but a late-night bottle shop
disgorges grubby plastic chairs, erodes a street corner.
        rumours and Europeans

shop king, he sweats, shirtless,
as fat as a toad. an empire of bottles
and chugging coolers. a plump-hand blaze.
the chiming register then pumping the scuffed
warm opener

having forsaken
(the myth of)   our Western recycling
we're basically paying to litter,
clinking bottles with plastic-chair strangers
beneath a hot, dark night
that would look away if it could

The Maldives

A is for *atoll*, a coral
island and ringed lagoon. nothing
that could remotely
pimple a hill,
let alone mountains.   specks
adrift in the Indian

B is for *bikini*, the French
swimsuit revolution named days after America's atomic
oceanic detonations.   the marketing:
global headlines and mushroom-cloud footage
forever exempting translation. a one-word
two-piece elegy for islets
bombed out of existence

C: the canaries in a very
global coal mine. where *metres above sea-level*
never hit triple digits. 1200 sneeze islands
halfway between Indonesia and Africa,
floating about an equator with no neighbours.
the pure
tiger horizon of predatory *Life of Pi*.
yet pale beaches as soft as cake
and pastry flour. ringed white
in the endless blue

a capital city so Muslim it's hard
to find a drink. an airport with a dock
but no bar.   disapproving
resort bartenders blindly follow recipes
they'll (probably) never taste as brother chefs
sizzle the guest bacon

the 'perfect' romantic getaway,
a bikini paradise with border police
who might turn you away for sex toys.
                a sinking island
with the world's highest divorce rate
will only tolerate
so many pleasures and explosions

Indonesia Is Burning, Gord, and I Don't Want To Breathe

our global ecocide tour, from the epitome of peak oil,
'our' Canadian tar sands,
to Indonesia's palm-oil gas ovens.
rubbing our sooty noses
in our world and species

Southeast Asia's annual fortnight without blue skies,
or moist eyes. thousands of slash-and-burn farmers
in Sumatra and Borneo ignite rainforest hectares
in the hundreds of thousands.   orangutans aflame,
all that streaking orange.   smothering
several countries in a Stephen-King fog,
thicker than Dickensian smog

Indonesia's late-summer cookout
of rainforests, elephants and peat,
smokes out the neighbours.   gassed Malaysia
and no-rich-island-is-not-an-island Singapore.
      snakes its grey all the way
to Thailand and the Philippines. tightens an acrid,
international scarf

that other burning Amazon, though this national
barrel fire is for food oil, not grazing beef.
the palm-oil tear gas attack of the world's biggest producer,
the career-pivot of Suharto's former death-squads,
purveyors of the world's lipstick, fried chicken
and dorm-room ramen.   all that
Lady-Macbeth soap

the sun not so much obliterated
as shunned, that Guernica lightbulb we don't want
glaring down on our grocery-store idiocy.   an accelerated
nightly gargle with a drier throat, a tighter
inner collar and the thin grey edge
of the lung-blackening wedge

no storm you've ever known, neither rain nor sleet nor hail,
has kept you inside this long,
no power outage.   two choked weeks, the opposite
of a tropical holiday

better, and worse, than the rolling wildfires
of California, Australia and BC, though the headaches
and hacked gasps have to ask
whether there's still a difference
between the fires we set to farm and the fires
our farms have set

And now Australia

refugees inside the island now,
not caged up by it.   flee the burning
Blue Mountains,
        Australia's Grand Canyon, but with trees,
that pit of Bruegel fire

half a billion roos, wallabies and dingoes
thrown on the planetary barbie. the first
crematorium of the sixth mass extinction. the forest
lost to fire bigger than West Virginia, that fellow
climate-change denier. the caustic
koala singe

a contest oligarchs but no people want to win:
        the most polluted
        air in the world. a smoke
plume wider than Europe and tireless
for the Tasman swim of thousands.   smothering
New Zealand's cool blue rivers, smudging those white
mountain-top glaciers,
smoking out the greenest
country on the planet

still more proof that in the climate crisis
we can run but not hide

a final cigarette
before the execution

Glossary

ang moh   Singaporean phrase, literally for
'redhead' but applied to all Caucasians, often with
derision if not hostility. Racial profiling
that doesn't answer to racial profiling (*cf.*
colonialism).

azan   The Muslim call to prayer
sung or broadcast from a minaret.

catch no ball   'doesn't understand.'

can   Anthem of a can-do people. Singaporean for 'can',
yes, but with much more enthusiasm than slacker
North America. Often a concluding response to
your proposal. Possibly half-aspirated (*cf.* the
inhaled Nova Scotian 'yeah'). Repeat for emphasis.
Can, can.

cannot   the buck stops here
along with your dumb idea
or any request
to bend the rules.

drop bomb   unexpected news. the striding
mistress we overheard screaming
into her cell and cutting the sidewalk air
with a sabre arm.
Now you drop bomb on me?

gahmen   Local pronunciation of 'government'
in a country that loves to save time, money and
even syllables.

kiasu   Hokkien for 'striving' esp. for excellence and/or to
not be left behind. Etymology: *kia* 'afraid' + *su*
'problem.'

kopi	Indonesian and Malay word for 'coffee.' Hallmark of a Singaporean *kopitiam* (*kopi* + *tiam*, Hokkien for 'shop'). Endless variations: *kopi gah dai, kopi kosong peng, kopi-O peng…*
lah	a Malay suffix added in Singapore for emphasis, caution, introspection, doubt, mockery or simply a verbal comma. Got more chill than the millennial *like*. E.g., 'No need. This one closing, lah.' Très grab-bag.
Singlish	This vibrant, beautiful language I can understand but not speak.
talking cock	A judgment used by surprisingly many, including tiny aunties, about, fittingly, someone bragging or being idiotic.
tuk-tuk	A scooter rickshaw with three wheels. Light automotive transport for 1-2 passengers. A soft enclosure, complete with two seats.　　　how you'll move anything in Thailand.　　　then your wife's perfect nickname for our second post-Asian dog, the puppy's fast, erratic darts and drive.

Thank You

scie scie

nandry

terima kasih

suksma

kop-khun-krub

cảm ơn bạn

shukuriyaa

akun

ta

kia ora

domo

Acknowledgements

The following literary festivals and centres provided chances to read many of these poems: the Ubud Writers and Readers Festival (Bali); the Dylan Thomas Birthplace (Swansea, Wales); the Australasian Association of Writing Programs conferences in Perth and Sydney; the Singapore Writers Festival; and the Georgetown Literary Festival (Penang, Malaysia).

I am grateful to Lasalle College of the Arts, Singapore, and the Canada Council for the Arts for the grants that made this book possible.

The poem "Angkor Wat" won the Banff Centre Bliss Carman Poetry Award, affording me the lifetime-high of a working week in the Baff Centre's Cardinal Studio. "Angkor Wat" was first published in *Prairie Fire*.

Other poems appear in the anthologies *Silence: The University of Canberra Vice-Chancellor's International Poetry Prize, 2019; Meridian: The APWT Drunken Boat Anthology of New Writing; Love the Words 2022*, from International Dylan Thomas Day and Infinity Books as well as *The Southeast Asian Review of English*.

In February of 2020, in Singapore, my recording of "Abandoned Bicycles" was featured in a multidisciplinary soundpainting performance by renowned French composer and choreographer Angélique Cormier.

The title "Chaos People" is borrowed from former Peace Corps volunteer Tom Bissell's story collection *God Lives in St. Petersburg and Other Stories*.

Cherian George's book *Air-Conditioned Nation: Essays about Singapore* inspired a title.

About the Author

Darryl Whetter is the author of eight books of fiction, poetry and creative nonfiction.

His most recent books are the climate-crisis novel *Our Sands*, from Penguin Random House (2020), and, as a creativity scholar and anthologist, *Teaching Creative Writing in Asia* (Routledge, 2022) and *Teaching Creative Writing in Canada* (Routledge, due in 2024).

His writing has been selected to various anthologies, including *Best Canadian Stories*, *Best Canadian Essays* and *Best Asian Short Stories*. His essays have been published by *The Brooklyn Rail*, *The Globe and Mail*, *The Detroit Times*, and *THIS Magazine*; and by Oxford University Press, Presses Sorbonne Nouvelle, and others.

Whetter has been a festival or campus author in Bali, Singapore, London, Penang, Swansea, Perth, Sydney and throughout his native Canada. He holds a PhD in literature and was recently the inaugural director of the first creative writing master's degree in Singapore, in a degree conferred by Goldsmiths, University of London.